'LIKE RO
STAKES I
A FOREST
CLEARING...'

RYSZARD KAPUŚCIŃSKI
Born 1932, Pińsk, Poland
Died 2007, Warsaw, Poland

Essays taken from *Nobody Leaves*, first published in English in 2017.

KAPUŚCIŃSKI IN PENGUIN MODERN CLASSICS
Another Day of Life
The Emperor
Nobody Leaves
The Shadow of the Sun
The Shah
Travels with Herodotus

RYSZARD KAPUŚCIŃSKI

An Advertisement for Toothpaste

Translated by William R. Brand

PENGUIN BOOKS

PENGUIN CLASSICS

UK | USA | Canada | Ireland | Australia
India | New Zealand | South Africa

Penguin Books is part of the Penguin Random House group
of companies whose addresses can be found at
global.penguinrandomhouse.com.

Penguin
Random House
UK

This selection first published 2018
001

Set in 11.2/13.75 pt Dante MT Std
Typeset by Jouve (UK), Milton Keynes
Printed in Great Britain by Clays Ltd, St Ives plc

ISBN: 978–0–241–33932–9

www.greenpenguin.co.uk

Contents

An Advertisement for Toothpaste

The sax wailed piercingly and Marian Jesion shouted: 'Let's go, boys.' On the forest road through the limitless darkness Jesion's grandmother sighed a tremulous whisper: 'Oh God.' Those three voices, raised simultaneously but so clearly out of step, weigh like a stone on the village of Pratki in Ełk county.

The girls from Pratki tell me that it was a lovely dance. The band came all the way from Olsztyn. Two people appeared with the band: a fantastic entertainer and a singer with fashionably teased hair, except that she was a bit too much on the scrawny side. The village hall had been swept and all the windows washed. The special effects came out great: red and blue light, filtered through rustling fronds of crepe paper, filled the hall. On the right wall, as seen from the door, it was more blue, whereas intense red flamed on the left. The girls stood on the blue side and the boys on the red side. They were divided by the multicoloured expanse of the village hall with the bandstand pinned in the middle like a brooch, but of course they could see each other clearly. There are fifteen girls in the village, and there are four boys. The girls saw how those boys stood stiffly in the romantic black of their suits, with plastic ties on elastic bands under their chins, the brilliantined masters of the world in wafts of Derby Eau de Cologne (produced by Lechia in Poznań). The boys looked pensively in the direction of the girls, evaluating the quality of their high heels, nylon dresses and Czech jewellery, as they mulled over all-too-predictable plans to be implemented later.

The girls told me that the saxophonist from Olsztyn, known throughout the province, started off by playing the hit of the season, titled 'Twenty-Four Thousand Kisses'. That hit is dazzling, and at the same time shocking. On hearing it, Marian Jesion shouted: 'Let's go, boys.'

But no one even moved a muscle.

A tension-filled hush descended.

The four boys glowed amaranthine on the left-hand side of the village hall, and the fifteen girls stood in shades of blue to the right. The cause of that tension-filled hush, into which the saxophonist known throughout the province wailed penetratingly, was obvious. It resulted from arithmetic. 15 to 4 is a good score in team handball, but it represents an atrocious disproportion at such an exceptionally glittering dance party (band from Olsztyn, great special effects).

The hush came from the red side, concentrating on making their choices, and emanated from the blue side, whose hope was as soundless as the silence of the stars. They all knew how many things in the village would depend on what happened in a moment, and so no one had any desire to make an ill-considered move. At last, the four on the left crossed over and enunciated the traditional formula to four of the ones on the blue side:

'Let's waltz, all right?'

The phrase 'all right' is absolutely rhetorical in nature here, added exclusively in order to lend the sentence a fluid cadence like something out of Sienkiewicz. If any of the girls replied: 'No', she would spend the rest of her days in a dubious state of spinsterhood. Therefore, the four from the blue side responded: 'Sure', and the couples moved into the centre. The saxophonist known throughout the province worked the gilded valves of his instrument and Marian Jesion shouted something in a loud voice. The saxophonist and his instrument had to play loudly enough to drown out the trembling whisper of Jesion's grandmother, who stood on the road amid the limitless darkness asking 'Oh Lord, why did he do this to me?'

The four couples performed their first turns. They were precisely calculated according to Euclidian and formalistic principles, like the timeless motions of the planets or the course of Sputniks around the earth. Those who remained on the blue side looked on with a mix of envy and criticism. Some of them deluded themselves that the soldiers would still show up. The soldiers came from Ełk – always the same ones. They were brought here by skinny, dark-haired Kazik, the corporal in charge of cultural affairs. Kazik had read many books and watched 700 movies. He entered every film in a notebook and totalled them up every quarter. By the end of his service, he might hit 800. Kazik, however, is treacherous, because he tells every girl the same thing. 'What does he say?' I ask.

They laugh, until one of them finally repeats it: 'Girl, I will drink delight from every cell of your body.'

He's from Warsaw, that Kazik, which is why he's such an intellectual. Soldiers are dangerous because they get carried away. They are on a pass that's good until ten o'clock and they want to close the deal in time. They have no regard for contemplation, and they dictate the tempo from the start. In such haste, a girl can forget herself, and after that nothing remains but death.

'What do you mean, death?' I ask.

'Really. What else is left for her? Only killing herself. The ones from Pratki are better, but even they fidget around too much.'

The saxophone croaked out the last bar of the hit and

the couples broke off their geometrical evolutions. The four boys standing against the wall went out behind the village hall, where they retrieved a flask hidden under a juniper bush. They drained it. The girls tell me that such is the custom and it's better that way, because it livens them up. Too much isn't good, but a little bit is good. The boys returned to the concrete-floored village hall and by their faces it looked like they had been under some enormous strain. In the hearts of the girls there again arose a hope as soundless as the silence of the stars.

Keeping pace with the latest achievements, the band known throughout the province launched into 'Diana', and the scarlet veins stood out on the skinny neck of the scrawny singer. The next four girls were led from the wall into the centre, where the red blended with the blue and settled into a respectable purple. Again the couples began absorbedly describing circles on the village-hall concrete to the beat of the song that the scrawny singer was enthusiastically belting out.

After that number, the girls tell me, the boys started pushing and shoving each other. They didn't know what that violent, predatory pushing and shoving was about. The girls think that if there's a fight at a dance, its purpose is not immediate, but rather more distant and somewhat metaphysical. It's necessary to make the dance memorable. A dance sinks into oblivion like a stone in the lake and the waters of time close over it. The dance itself is coarse and boorish, and too many factors prevent it from living on. With a fight there are no inhibitions, and it lives on in full. A fight has everything that sticks in human memory: blood, pain, eyes fixed in hatred, the prickly thrill of death. The village will rehash the details of the fight, and the names of the participants will be repeated many times.

During the quick waltz that followed the fight, the couples adopted a style ordained by the fantastic entertainer. They passed in front of the band with the step that's obligatory during the Sunday promenade. The girls tell me that the promenade takes place every Sunday afternoon in the village. First the boy shows up at the girl's house and asks: 'Want to promenade with me?' The girl must introduce him to her father and the father must converse with the boy. On this occasion the beau opens a flask, because dry conversation is like goose down in a gale. This legalizes the act of promenading. They walk along the road from house number one to the last house in the village, and back. They can't go into the woods, because that's disapproved of. From time to time during the fulfilment of this sterile and tedious procedure, a word is uttered.

'So what do you talk about?' I asked.

One of them replied: 'This and that.'

On this basis I could not deduce whether these conversations are interesting or boring, because I do not possess the Egyptological talent that can derive the stormy history of a dynasty from a single hieroglyph.

In the opinion of the girls, their friends in other villages, where the balance of the sexes is not so glaringly disproportionate, are better off because they can be choosy. They can be choosy when it comes to boys. When he comes along with his invitation to go globe-trotting, the girl first asks him: 'Are you going to move to the city or stay on the farm?' If he intends to stay on the farm, the girl sends him away: 'Go promenade by yourself.'

With a boy like that, there's no hope of getting out of the village, and all the girls want to move to the city.

'Why?' I ask.

'Because in the city there are so many cinemas, and people don't have to do things.'

'But on the other hand it's dangerous in the city,' I say. 'There are lots of accidents.'

'So? We have accidents here too. Not long ago one girl was going to feed the chickens, and she slipped and broke her arm. That's an accident, too.'

The fantastic guy known throughout the province performed his routines. He managed to conjure a flag out of thin air and hung it on a specially prepared pole.

The band played the national anthem and the scrawny singer stood at attention on stage. That was the last waltz, the end of the planetary revolutions, and the metaphorical significance of the red and blue was no more. The door of the village hall opened and four snuggling couples walked out into the tunnel of the night. A moment later, the group of stiff, silent, resentful girls followed in their trail. These were the eleven not chosen, abandoned to the predations of loneliness, neglect, and the night – that same night in which Jesion's grandmother, at the end of her strength, managed to whisper on the forest road: 'Oh God, why did he . . .'

And she fainted.

A police van took grandmother to the old people's home in Nowa Wieś, outside Ełk. Now she sits on a bench, rubbing the knee that is swollen from her fall on the road. 'No,' she lisps, 'he didn't throw me out. He only said: "Grandmother is leaving the village." ' In itself, the sentence does not sound threatening. It's more like something out of a primer, descriptive and narrative: Grandmother is leaving the village. Why did he say this to his grandmother? Grandmother thinks it over: 'Because there's not much room in the cottage and my grandson, you see, Marian Jesion, is going to get married. The need has come over him. That's what he told me: "Grandmother, the need has come over me." '

That's why, on that evening when there was a beautiful dance party with very impressive special effects, Jesion's grandmother set out into the vortex of darkness, walking straight ahead into the unknown, into the world. Grandmother entered into the darkness, and her grandson, Marian Jesion, in his romantic black suit, the brilliantined master of the world in clouds of Derby Eau de Cologne (produced by Lechia, Poznań), danced to the dazzling and at the same time shocking hit of the season, 'Twenty-Four Thousand Kisses', piercingly wailed by the saxophonist known throughout the province.

And everything's the way it should be.

Marian Jesion will ease his excruciating need, and his grandmother will have a government roof over her head and a government bowl of bean soup with bacon. What will change is this: because there will be one less mouth to feed in the Jesion household, expenses will be reduced and Marian, with all his needs, will be able to buy himself a plastic tie on an elastic band. This is unquestionably a symbol of modernity, and in Pratki there is a big turning towards modernity. My girls tell me that people are now buying everything: sewing machines, WFM motorcycles, sofas and watches. People are striving after radios, suits, crystal and washing machines. In strict confidence, the girls tell me that some people, in order to keep up with this universal inclination to material prosperity, are simply stealing. And so for instance the cooks at the nearby collective farm steal meat. How clever they are! They sneak ham and pork cheeks out in pails of slop. Then they just rinse the meat at the well and the whole village can buy it. Hence on a fine Sunday the sly cooks can adorn their bell-shaped bosoms in the blue mist of expensive chiffon blouses.

'Do you know that stealing is a sin?' I ask.

My charming girls from Pratki laugh, but it's not a natural laugh, pearly and dazzling, but rather a grotesque, clownish grimace of a laugh in which their lips stretch from ear to ear but remain clamped tightly shut, and their insides seem to shake autonomously in a hysterical convulsion. They have to laugh that way because they have no teeth, or, more precisely, they have a few teeth, scattered here and there, sparsely, like rotting stakes in a forest clearing.

As badly brought up, as notorious a boor as I am, I ask my girls: 'Why don't you gals brush your teeth?' But why ask about that? Nobody in Pratki brushes their teeth. Pratki girls chew that ham with devastated, bare gums, and the boys, after downing a glass of moonshine, ruminate like old men over a mouthful of pickles. Pratki bachelors buy themselves motorcycles and the girls acquire, for a pretty penny, fashionable organdie slips, which is why nobody can afford a tube of Odonto toothpaste (produced by Lechia, Poznań) for three zloty and five grosz. It immediately occurred to me to launch a campaign to lower the price of toothpaste, and particularly to roll back the retail price by those five grosz, because maybe that's what discourages people from an excessive, budget-straining purchase when they are set on buying themselves a collection of crystal. I counted on lining up a cohort of backers; the whole issue would meet with a favourable response in the Ministry. Steps would be taken and, with a special directive, that five-grosz barrier would be rescinded once and for all.

But later I came to a different understanding. If they don't brush their teeth, and the idea of such a procedure has never even entered their heads, they could hardly be interested in the price of Odonto toothpaste (produced by Lechia, Poznań), amounting to 3.05 zloty, or take into consideration the fact of those five grosz that were overzealously added to the round sum of three zloty. The hygienic principle under discussion is ignored because not a word has been said to the people of Pratki in this regard, and no one in the village has independently and spontaneously stumbled upon the idea of brushing their teeth.

And that's the whole truth.

Namely, the truth is that Pratki dances to the newest, dazzling hits, races all over the place on WFMs, stocks up on televisions, purchases electric sewing machines and Master Picasso curtains, while at the same time the idol of Pratki is still an idiot known throughout the province who is a fantastic entertainer, and at the same time Pratki forces a sick old lady out into the unknown, gets into brawls and foams at the mouth with hatred, and doesn't brush its teeth.

Thinking in these terms, I slipped immediately into idealism and started dreaming. I dreamed that, at the cost of playing three dance records, some responsible person on the radio would say a few words about teeth. That you have to put the toothpaste on the toothbrush, and then you have to rub it in with a back-and-forth rotational motion, and afterwards you have to spit it out instead of swallowing it. That there are hopes for a reduction in the price of a single tube to three zloty. I went on to dream that the country instructor sitting in at the next Party meeting, after discussing the critical issues in the ongoing flourishing of our fatherland, would deign to ask, in spite of himself and out of nowhere: 'And how about those teeth, comrades? Are you brushing those teeth or not?'

Because sewing machines and nylon ties have been exported to Pratki, chiffon blouses and convertible sofas, but no one has gone to the trouble of inculcating a few elementary concepts from the domain of elementary culture.

Grandmothers, and teeth.

Apparently two different matters, but not quite entirely.

Danka

I started at the rectory. I knocked on the massive door.
The lock grated, the keys jangled, and at last the door
handle moved slightly. The oval of a wary face loomed
out of the shadowy vestibule and froze.

'I wanted to speak with the priest.'

'You are?'

'I'm from the press, and I travelled here . . .'

'I thought so. Of course. I understand. Unfortunately,
Father is not here. I've disappointed you, haven't I? Were
you counting on something spicy? My God, it could
almost be funny.'

'When will Father be home?'

'Oh, that doesn't depend on you or on me. It's for
others to decide. Let's not speculate.'

The face receded into the shadows, the key jangled
again, the lock grated again. The rectory stood at the
end of a lane that began at the town square. It stood near
the lake, in a cloud of maples and oaks, two storeys high,
banal and plain in its architecture. Next to it, above the

tops of the trees, rose the church spire with its gallery and bell. A little house, a small, colourful cottage, squatted further on, but still within the bounds of the parish property. That must be where they lived, I thought. I approached it to check whether the windows in the cottage were broken. Yes, they were broken.

I went back into the town. I won't give its name, and the reportage will explain why. It lies in the northern part of Bialystok province, and there is no one who has not seen, at least once in their life, one of a hundred little towns like this. There's nothing distinctive about any of them. They put on a drowsy face, damp patches growing with lichens in the furrows of their crumbling walls, and anyone who walks across the town square has the impression that everything is staring at him insistently from under half-closed, motionless eyelids.

The town square is cobblestone, rectangular and empty. It's raining. All of July has been streaming with rain and people have stopped believing in summer. And the little town is dripping with rain, the roofs and the lanes and the sidewalks. A few young trees growing on the square are also dripping with rain. Under the trees stands a youngster. He's wearing a jacket in a broad check, authentic jeans and worn-out sneakers. He's standing there without purpose or hope just for the sake of standing there, just to keep going and survive somehow, like the ones who stand in front of the Central Department Store, for whom standing is a form of existence, a lifestyle, a pose, and a game.

I asked him: 'Are you from here?'

'Not now. Now I'm from Warsaw.'

'On holiday?'

'You got it.'

We went to the inn. There was a restaurant in one room and a coffee shop in the other. The smoke hung low, in woolly grey streaks. The waiter brought wine.

'What's all this about?' asked the youngster.

I started in on the business with the rectory. Maybe he knew something? Maybe he was there?

'No way,' he said. 'When I got in from Warsaw it was all over. Not much to say, just a lot of talk. The guys told me about how those old biddies went there. She's in the hospital now. She was supposedly out of this world. Legs to dream of, stacked, a pretty face, everything in the right place. Ones like that come along, and you have to move fast. I picked up a girl like that in the spring. Jesus, talk about lovely! From Śniadeckich, do you know the street? I go to the Polytechnic there. Just a kid, sweet sixteen, but wow, nothing more to say. When a man has time on his hands, that's great, but what can you do when they make you hit the books? You can't get away with it. Don't waste your time on the scandal. It's just a shame about the girl. But people here have no orientation. Is it any wonder?'

He advised me: 'Talk to the boss of the restaurant. She always knows what's up.'

He went off and came back with the lady. She was a stout woman, dressed with exaggerated, awkward elegance. Her face was slathered with powder, rouge and lipstick. She sat down, leaning her elbows on the table and twirling her fingers in her hair.

'I went along, of course,' she said. 'My business requires it. Personally, I wouldn't have gone, but I had to for the sake of my business. If I had said no, the women would have forbidden their husbands to set foot in my restaurant. Then I lose customers and the municipal hotel takes them. The hotel has a restaurant, too. So when they started gathering in front of the house that's now being built near the fire station, I left my husband to mind the place and went there. At first there were plans to seize the priest, but he was gone because they'd summoned him to the curia. Then somebody shouted that we should go into the church and beseech God not to take revenge on us for the affront committed in his holy sanctuary. When we went inside – have you seen the church already? – that figure was standing in the middle with wood chips all around it, because she's wooden, and she wasn't ready yet. So we all knelt down, but old

Sadowska jumped to her feet and screamed: "Chop her up. Chop her up and burn her. Get her out of our sight." That's what she screamed. And she ran up to that figure, and there were various mallets lying around, and a chisel and a hatchet, and she waved it around, and I felt a chill. She struck it once, but Florkowa came flying after her, the one with the son who works at the mill, and she caught Sadowska by the arm and said: "Drop that hatchet, don't you even dare to touch that figure, because it's holy." And Sadowska shouts: "Holy? She's a harlot, not holy." She said even worse things but I'm not going to repeat them. You know. And Florkowa shouts back at her: "Don't blaspheme, because hell will swallow you up and us too for condoning it." At which Sadowska turned around to face us, and we, we're all kneeling there and our legs are leaden with fear, and she cries out: "Look, you women, don't be blind. Look, if it's not that harlot. It's her after all, may the earth cover me, it's her." And I'm telling you, but don't breathe a word because it'll be the end of me – it was her. The head, the face, the figure – the exact same. Identical. And at that moment each of us felt such dread, such madness, that none of us dared to back Sadowska up. And Florkowa stood there shielding the figure and saying, "Over my dead body. Over my dead body." And it was, sir, a beautiful day, not like today, except that in the church it was grey, gloomy, heavy with fear and the screaming of those women. Sad-owska broke down sobbing, howling, and we began slipping out of the door. And what do you know, as we're leaving, out of that little cottage next to the rectory comes the girl herself. Mother of God! I, of course, I'm not backward in terms of fashion, I've been to Sopot and I myself dress *très chic*. But nobody here had ever seen anything like that. And our priest himself used to rail against depravity until it made you quake. He forbade girls to play volleyball. I myself don't know what's come over him now. I try to figure it out, but I just don't know. So that girl comes up to us and she's wearing a bathing suit, what do you call it, a bikini. A man sneezes and everything flies away. You know, sir, women don't like saying good things about each other, but I'm not back-ward and I'll admit that girl was like a rose blossom. Any man would go through torments and purgatory for one like her. Good Lord, sir, the women see her and you can hear them hissing. If she'd just kept going then maybe nothing would have happened, or if she'd crossed our path some other day then maybe nothing would have happened either, but we had just come out of church and there had been that scene in there that I told you about, and every one of us had a heart full of terror and bitterness that we wanted to get rid of. The girl came up to us and asked, "Are you ladies looking for somebody?"

At that point Maciaszkowa stepped forward and said, "Yes. You, you pestilence!" And wham! over the head with her cane, because Maciaszkowa has trouble walking and uses a cane. And then she let her have it a second and a third time. I stood there like a stone, sir, and everything went black before my eyes and I thought: What's going on, what's going on, and my thoughts jumbled in my head like magpies in a tree hollow. They're laying into her and I don't move a muscle. Then afterwards they went over to that cottage, smashed the windows, and dragged out the furniture and broke it up, even though the furniture belonged to the priest. At that moment I look up and I see Michal coming, that is, our church sexton. I call out to the women and they run for it, with me behind them. I already told them at the police station that my business requires me to always go with the people. I'm not backward, but I had to go.'

The police station is also located on the town square, across from the inn. It's easy to see from there what condition the regulars are in when they emerge. They can be marched straight across to the opposite side of the square, where they can sober up and recover their equilibrium under lock and key. The policeman on duty sits behind the railing observing the square, and he says: 'In general, things are calm here. But there was one incident. We never had anything like that happen before.'

'Yes, exactly,' I break in. 'I'm interested in the details.'

He smiles in a vague sort of way because he wouldn't want to talk without permission from the chief. An hour later I'm leafing through a dossier full of material that I obtained from the station chief. The chief is eagerly assisting me, suggesting names and providing addresses. I search the papers strewn across the desk and he keeps pulling new ones out of the folder.

'I state that Citizen Helena Krakowiak my neighbour came to me first, and stated enough already of these scenes of depravity spreading through the vicinity, the Lord Jesus himself drove the moneylenders out of the church thus setting an example for us. She also stated of her own accord that we give money on the collection plate, taking it out of the mouths of our children, and they fatten themselves on it in order to commit ignominy. We have already looked on this for a month and our patience is exhausted and how long are we going to look on this sight, indicated Citizen Helena Krakowiak, may their offspring go to the devil, and she crossed herself. The above-named stressed that a figure of Our Lady could have been bought for the money collected and then there would not have been an affront to morality and debauchery such as the world has never seen. Next I would like to submit that other citizens also came to me, that is' – numerous names here – 'asserting their agreement with the above-named citizen who dropped a hint about driving out that prostitute as she expressed it because we have no need of whores in the rectory, as she also said. The above-named women stated that there was no other way out and Citizen Helena Krakowiak indicated a place near the fire station on the date of Tuesday, 28 June, at the time of four o'clock in the afternoon in order to be able to give the men and children dinner, wash the dishes and put them away . . .'

Later that day, I spoke with the secretary of the Municipal Committee. Tall and sinewy, he sat facing me, slumping his broad shoulders. He wiped his forehead, considered things, and enunciated his sentences slowly, with forethought.

'You are aware, comrade, that this might have been a provocation after all.'

'By which side?' I asked.

'By the clergy. The clergy likes doing such things whenever we try to see what they're up to.'

He stuck to this statement and refused to admit any other version. It must have been a provocation, he repeated. I didn't know the priest, but he knew him. The priest made moves that were very telling. You only had to analyse them. Their sense was clear. Perfectly clear.

We changed the subject. The new subject pleased him, and me. A factory was being built in town. They were already digging the foundations, and they were also going to build a housing settlement. The little town would get moving and play a new role. It would find its place on the economic map of the country. Even today its future already looked promising. I made a pledge to come and do a report. We shook hands and again I was walking the street, the rain was falling, the water was murmuring in the gutters, and that guy in jeans was standing under the trees on the square. It was he who suggested that I should meet with the sexton, and who led me through a hole in the fence, down a passageway and through the yard. The dwelling that we entered was crowded with beds and chairs, and the walls were covered with pictures and satirical caricatures from magazines published in Warsaw. Two men were sitting at the table. One was older, with his arm in a sling, and the other was blond, robust and tall – his son, as it turned out. The old man stood up and went out.

'My father's sick,' said the blond man, 'his arm just won't heal. I'm staying here to help him, because we also have a little land, but I'm dying to leave for the big city!' Michal S. finished his military service and when he came home the old sexton had died, and they took him as his replacement. There's no other work to be found, at least until they build that factory. I could tell that he didn't take his position very seriously, he'd seen a little bit of the world, and would change jobs at the first opportunity.

'Are you here about that brawl?' He chuckled at my interest in it. It was starting to get dark, the rain was falling, and water ran down the windows. 'I could make tea,' Michal offered.

'It was May when he came here. I was trimming the trees. A man walks up and asks about the priest. He wasn't over thirty, dressed in a sweater with a kerchief tied around his neck, and he was holding a package. I led him into the parish office. He said hello and introduced himself. He said he was a sculptor from Wroclaw. He unwrapped the parcel, and there was the head of a woman. "Take a look at it," he said. "It's a plaster sculpture of the Virgin Mary. Won't you think about it, Father?" Our old man started studying it, picked it up, judged its weight, and then said no, he wouldn't take it. The other one took the head and wrapped it back up, but then the old man told him to sit down and began questioning him about where he studied, what he was doing, whether he had had any exhibitions, and similar details. It was plain that the old man liked him, because he said: "You know, I'm not going to buy that Virgin Mary, but our little church was remodelled in the spring, we restored the side altar, and we need a statue of the Blessed Mother there. There used to be one, but the termites got to it so bad that it fell to pieces. Maybe you could do one." The other man said: "Of course", and so they went to look at the place. The sculptor figured and figured and then he said: "Well then, five thousand and it'll be all right." The old man protested. He didn't have the money, the remodelling had cleaned him out and he couldn't give that much. They haggled until the priest tried a new tack: "Let's do it another way," he says. "I've got a cottage for the sexton here but he lives in town, and so the cottage is standing vacant. You live there, I'll feed you, and you make me that sculpture. There's a lake here, the forest, a beautiful setting." The sculptor didn't say anything, you could see that he was working something out, and then he responded: "All right, Father, but on one condition. Right now I'm working on a sculpture that's very important to me, and I can't break off. I'm doing that sculpture with a model. So I'll accept your proposal if you permit me to live here with my model." The old man was taken aback and cried out: "Here, in the rectory!?" I looked at him and I could see that he was getting cold feet. He didn't want to do it, he didn't want to do it, but he's tight-fisted and in the end he said: "It's a deal."

'They arrived at the beginning of June. That was when I saw her. She wasn't a woman. She was a miracle. Graceful, lovely, fair-haired. She introduced herself to me and said, "My name's Danka. And you?" I couldn't get the words out. My throat tightened up, I saw stars, and I thought I was dying. I mumbled something, but then I immediately thought: "Michal, strange things are going to start happening around here." And look – I was right.

At first the old man stayed out of her way. He sat indoors and didn't come out. And she acts like she's on the beach – she strips down, blanket on the grass, and sunbathes. In her bathing suit all the time from morning till night. Believe me, you were almost afraid to look at her. Because when you looked, you wanted to cry because you were such a nothing, such an accursed zero, and you could howl until the end of the world and she'd never even glance at you. That sculptor followed her around like a puppy. He had to love her, to love her for all the men who weren't allowed to. He was OK, a very decent guy. I helped him find wood, I sharpened his instruments, and more than once I went into town to buy wine for them. We got along. As soon as there was wood, he set right to work. He had a steady hand and he carved boldly, skilfully. That was when the old man started coming out of the rectory. He would weave in and out between the trees, and Danka was lying on the blanket. The old man wanted to get closer, but then he would immediately back away. It tempted him, but he held out. I watched him sometimes and I wanted to laugh. She would stand up and wanted to go over to him, but the old man would dash into the church. Like a game of cat and mouse. She gave him a hell of a time. He often looked in on the sculptor to see how the work was progressing. He sat down on the bench, looked around, and didn't say anything at first. Only when he started carving the face did the old man enter into longer talks with him. I would also go in to look at the sculpture, and I saw what was going on. He was carving Danka. He carved her face, her neck, her shoulders. Further down it was a long robe, but from there up it was Danka. The old man would ask if the mouth wasn't too wide. Because she had small lips, full, but small. I got the feeling that he wanted that Virgin Mary at the altar to be the image of Danka. But he couldn't come right out and say it.

'And in town it was already buzzing like a beehive. Guys came running to have a look, and the women gathered, supposedly to pray. It got busy around the rectory. Talking, rumours, speculation all at once, as you please. They kept asking me, too: "Michal, who is she?" And I told them the truth, because a person is stupid. A couple of women came as a delegation to the priest. He explained something to them and it was quiet for a few days. Then it started up again and got worse. At one point they summoned the old man to the curia, just when that sculptor went to Bialystok to get a chisel. And that's when those hags came around.'

Michal S. wasn't there. Afterwards, he helped take her to the hospital. When he came back, he told everything to the one man in town who had befriended the sculptor – Józef T., who taught Polish at the school.

Józef T. (I call on him late at night) says: 'We were sitting around late in the evening. "It was at the seashore, a couple of years ago," the sculptor told me. "I was looking for a subject for my diploma work. I wandered around the beach and the days flew by. It's easier to find a model at the beach than in the city, because people are undressed. I didn't come across anything interesting. Once I was walking along the water's edge, it was an empty spot, a fishing boat pulled up on the sand was rotting away. I went over to it, and a girl was sitting behind the boat. She asked: 'Do you have to stand right there?' 'If you could see yourself, you wouldn't ask such questions,' I replied. We were very young, and that was the prevailing form in those days. A month later, Danka came to Wroclaw with me, to my garret. I sculpted her there. The title of the work was supposed to mean something, so I named the statue 'Girl After Work' and took it to the exhibition. The jury rejected it. They said it was too sacral. I was shattered, I couldn't get my bearings. I lay on the bed for hours in a complete stupor. Finally

I got a crazy idea. I borrowed a cart from the doorman, packed up the sculpture and went to the diocesan curia. I told them: 'Buy this, it's a piece called "The Madonna Anticipating the Annunciation."' They conferred, but in the end they didn't take it. It was too socialist realist, they said. I couldn't stand any more. I dragged the cart to the Oder River and smashed the plaster with a hammer. Because it was plaster. When I came to my senses, I saw that the head of the sculpture was still there. I wanted to throw it into the river. I didn't do it. I took it with me. I carried it to the studio and dumped it in the corner.

'"It was only this year that I ran into Danka again. Everything was like before. 'Come on, let's go to the Mazury,' I told her. She agreed. But I didn't have a grosz to my name. Then I remembered that head. I thought: I'll take it along, I'll fob it off on some priest, and by the way I'll find a place to hole up. That's how I ended up here."'

And today is Sunday. It's raining, and the rain will probably never stop falling. A flood. A deluge. People are losing their homes. Severe economic damage. Out of the window of the little hotel I can see how, despite the puddles, the residents of the little town are coming out into the street and, in their Sunday best, walking at a dignified pace towards the square, to the inn or to the church. I get dressed and go out. I already know some of the faces.

We bow to each other. A reporter can't hide for long. So I don't duck into the hidden passageways but walk down the main street, which is busy and deep in mud.

I enter the church. In the glimmer of the candles stands a wooden statue, the figure of a lovely girl. It's an unfinished work, but the master has already managed to render the face, head and shoulders in detail. These are details of the highest order. People come up, kneel, bend their backs. I hold my head up high. I can't take my eyes off it.

The Taking of Elżbieta

'Sister,' I asked, 'why did you do it, Sister?'

We were kneeling in the snow, under a low sky, with an iron grille between us. Through the grille I saw the eyes of the nun, big eyes, brown, with fever in the irises. She was silent, looking off to the side. People who look off to the side have something to say, but fear gags their throat. Then I heard her voice:

'What have you brought me?'

But I had nothing. I had neither any words nor any things. I came here alone, waded in the snow through the forest, knocked at the convent gate, and in the end stood before the steep grille bearing the one single question that I had already asked. And it had disappeared into the stiff folds of the habit, without an echo.

That is why I retorted:

'I really don't know. Perhaps only your mother's scream.'

That scream roused the village each night. Drowsy from their overheated duvets, dreams and love, the women got out of bed. They stood cautiously at the windows. They could see only the darkness. Therefore they told their husbands: 'Go and see what's out there.' The peasants stuffed their feet into their rubber boots and went outside. They walked sleepily, caressing the darkness with their hands, as if the scream were something you could take hold of like a sheaf of rye and press down to the ground with your knee. In the end, at the holy figure, they found a tall, skinny woman in an old overcoat. The woman was coughing. She had a sunken chest and was holding her arms as if she were waiting to greet someone dear to her. But she enfolded in those arms not someone's life, but her own death. She carried tuberculosis within herself. The peasants told the woman: 'Why are you whimpering in the night? Go and sleep.' Relieved that it wasn't a murder, or a break-in, or a fire, but only ordinary pain, and not their pain after all, they returned to the warmth of the duvet, sleep, and women's bodies.

Later, that skinny woman with her shoulders in an arc was taken to the hospital, because in that scream of hers there was also blood. Now the village could sleep amidst the silence, and the peasants stopped feeling the darkness with their hands. After three months, the woman returned. People saw that her eyes were now dry and stony, and the first night they realized that there was no screaming in her lungs. The village that had previously feared the screaming now dreaded the silence. The silence drew people in like deep water. They began going around to see the woman. They entered the cottage, which was like all the other cottages in the village – with a bouquet of artificial flowers, with a tinted wedding photograph, and with a gypsum dancing girl with a daintily modelled bust. The tall woman opened the wardrobe and showed them the row of dresses hanging there. Colourful dresses, cheap and banal, because, my Lord, this was hardly Paris. She said: 'She did not permit me to destroy these dresses. She pleaded: "Mama, I'll come back." '

Then the husband of that tall woman begged her: 'Stop. Just stop.'

The man lay in bed, absorbed in listening to his own heart. His heart had been struck by a second attack, and so he lay there motionless and listened. The listening was enough to make him break out in a sweat, because it was full of tension and effort. What it feels like, Mr Reporter, is that I'm not listening to the present beat, but for the one that should come next. Will I hear it, or will there be silence?

So he lies there motionless, with hypertension – 250 – preoccupied with his own heart and nothing else, because the heart itself is a whole world, and no person can encompass two worlds at the same time. He's already lived his life, this man with two heart attacks. He's done day labour and regular jobs, and been in a camp and in prison. He and that tall woman had one child, their daughter Elżbieta. Elżbieta was born in 1939, a month before the war. The Germans put the husband behind barbed wire, and the tall woman was left by herself. She went out to dig beets. That work exhausts your strength because the soil that beets grow in is heavy soil. The mother laid Elżbieta down between the furrows, in the shade of the lush leaves. She herself dug in the sunshine, out of breath and coughing. Her arms dropped to her side. In the evenings she made extra money by writing letters to their boyfriends for the girls. 'In the first words of my letter I wish to ask you, dear Władek, if you know whether your feelings pulse with the same sentiment as earlier but if there is no lessening in your intransigence then mine towards you is the same, of which I am informing you.' For a letter like this, she received three eggs, and if it was a letter in which the passion was supposed to explode with flaming power, then she got a hen.

The father returned after the war and, as it often was in those years, the child had to learn to say 'Daddy' to a stranger. But he was no stranger to the mother of this child. Nothing came of this meeting after a long separation. Elżbieta became an only child. She started going to school, and later to high school. The man with two heart attacks and the tall woman are simple people. They know nothing about the Platonic system or the fact that Shakespeare was great and Mozart died cursing the world. But they saw an exhibition of books in a small town and perhaps someone told them that there are people in the world who have a lot of things in their head, and that such people are treated with respect. That was why they wanted Elżbieta to study. But the man with the two heart attacks could not work, and the tall woman had only a pension. And she also had tuberculosis. It was a good thing, that woman told me, that I had tuberculosis, because when I got medicine from the outpatient clinic I sold it on the sly so that I could give Elżbieta what she needed.

Elżbieta passed her final school exam in 1957 and became a schoolteacher. A good teacher, going by her reputation. I pick up a picture taken in those days. In this picture, Elżbieta is smiling, but the man with two heart attacks and the tall woman stand there very solemn. They are solemn because they are bursting with pride. Leave aside for a moment your admiration for the creators of electronic machines, for the constructors of rockets and the builders of new cities. Think about the mother who left her lungs to rot and the father who wore out his heart so that their daughter could become a teacher.

Elżbieta is a teacher and now she will go to university. But Elżbieta does not go to university. In 1961, she joins the order. The blow was crushing, it was murderous. The mother wandered along the road at night and the woken-up peasants caressing the darkness with their hands finally found the tall woman at the edge of exhaustion and then, relieved that it wasn't a murder, or a break-in, or a fire, but only ordinary pain and not their pain after all, they returned to their cottages and the warmth of the duvet, sleep, and women's bodies.

The tall woman was left alone. She was no stranger to solitude. Even when Elżbieta was going to high school, the sisters were drawing her in. At Elżbieta's home it was cold, the pot was empty, and her mother lay there spitting clots. At the nuns' it was warm and they fed her well. She sat there whole days.

Later I asked: 'Sister, in those times did any of the nuns ask the sister whether her mother had a glass of water at her bedside?'

She responded: 'No.'

'And did any of the nuns tell the sister: "Daughter, before you come to us to nibble at the chicken, at least bake your mother some potatoes in their jackets"?'

She responded: 'No.'

'Thank you,' I said, in order to maintain civility within the framework of general state policy towards the Church.

After her final exam, the nuns stepped up their pressure on Elżbieta. She was an affectionate girl, introverted and submissive. Her mother said there was something strange about her. She would have attacks of fear and cry.

'What did they tell her?' I asked the tall woman. They talked to her in general terms, which is always dangerous. The word condemnation, and the word eternal, and the word remember, and the word accursed. Elżbieta came home with a fever. I recited to the mother Éluard's poem about Gabriel Péri:

> *There are words that give life*
> *And they are innocent words*
> *The word fire and the word trust*
> *Love, justice, and the word freedom*

No, she answered. None of those words. In the end, Elżbieta disappeared from home. The first letter that arrived from the convent began with the salutation 'Through Mary to Jesus!' There are several of these letters. I sense the hand of the censor upon them, but telling phrases nevertheless slip through, such as 'I beseech you O Lord to give me the grace to persevere to the end.' Or 'Have you already excluded me from your memory? I beg you not to do so.'

The tall woman wanted to fight. With what weapons can a woman like that fight? All that she had was the X-ray of her lungs. I look over that smoky image of the coal-black cavity. With that film, the tall woman travelled halfway across Poland to the convent. The Mother Superior, who was not a doctor, picked up the X-ray, looked it over, and burst out laughing. 'There's nothing there!'

The mother came home but her husband was gone. Her husband was in the hospital. He had suffered that second heart attack. The doctors doubted that he would make it. The mother sent Elżbieta a letter, asking her to come at once. But Elżbieta never showed up. The letter was not delivered to her. Instead of her, two nuns appeared in the hospital where her father lay unconscious, to check whether there was really anything wrong with him. 'Is one of you sisters the daughter of the patient?' the department head asked.

'No, we've been sent here,' they replied, and withdrew their faces into the shadows of their starched wimples.

And so the mother sent a letter to the Primate of Poland. I read that letter, too. I also read the reply. It is a little correspondence form, on the letterhead of the chancellery of the primate, which states that 'accusations directed at this office are untrue and we advise you to keep quiet'. It strikes me that this is not bad advice. After all, it's a good thing to remain quiet in cases of tuberculosis and heart trouble. I also think that centuries of experience have gone into this reply, and that it's even known what kind of experience this has been. I may also think one thing or another, but what I think has no significance here. I can say that I feel sorry for that tall woman and that man with blood pressure of 250. I feel sorry for those peasant men whose sleep was interrupted and who went out caressing the darkness with their hands, as if the scream that came out of the darkness were something that could be grasped in a handful like sheaves of rye and crushed down on the ground under their knees. That woman and that man did not have much of a life, although they gave it their lungs and their heart. After that, they tried to fight. But when solitary people try to fight for their cause, it is only at that moment when they naively forget that right must yield to might. In the end, that moment always passes. And what's left is what's left.

That is why I told Elżbieta: 'I really don't know what I've brought you. Maybe only your mother's scream.'

And that scream, which after all cannot be taken by the handful like a sheaf of rye and pressed to the ground under your knee, seems to me something completely real. I could hear it, see it and touch it. It was authentic, even if it lasted but a moment. Many people heard it and those people knew why that tall woman screamed.

Those people could reflect upon it. And that's a lot, if you really do reflect upon it.

Standing at the grille, Elżbieta and I were silent. Nuns started coming down the stairs. First there were three of them, then five, and finally I stopped counting. They moved Elżbieta to the rear. In the end I couldn't see her. I saw many unmoving faces, but the face of Elżbieta Trębaczyk, a teacher from outside Kalisz, was gone.

And so I turned around and walked back in the snow, through the forest, to the station.

The Stiff

The truck is racing through the dusk, its headlamps, like a pair of eyes, searching for the finish line. It's close: Jeziorany, twenty kilometres. Another half-hour and we'll be there. The truck is pushing hard, but it's touch and go. The old machine wasn't meant for such a long haul.

On the flatbed lies a coffin.

Atop the box is a garland of haggard angels. It's worst on bends: the box slides and threatens to crush the legs of those sitting on the side rails.

The road bends into blind curves, climbing. The engine howls, rises a few notes, hiccups, chokes, and stops. Another breakdown. A smeared figure alights from the cab. That's Zieja, the driver. He crawls under the truck, looking for the damage. Hidden underneath, he swears at the perverse world. He spits when hot grease drips onto his face. Finally he drags himself out into the middle of the road and brushes off his clothes. '*Kaput,*' he says. 'It won't start. You can smoke.'

To hell with smoking. We feel like crying.

Just two days ago I was in Silesia at the Aleksandra-Maria coal mine. The story called for an interview with the director of the workers' dormitory. I found him in his office explaining something to six stocky youngsters. And I listened in.

This was the problem. During blasting, a block of coal had fallen and crushed a miner. They managed to dig out the body, but it was badly smashed. No one had known the dead man well. He had been working in the mine for barely two weeks. His identity was established. Name: Stefan Kanik. Age: eighteen. His father lived in Jeziorany, in Mazuria. The management contacted the local authorities there by telephone. It turned out that the father was paralysed and could not travel to the funeral. The Jeziorany authorities asked if the remains couldn't be transported to the home town. The management agreed, provided a truck, and assigned the director of the workers' dormitory to find six people to escort the coffin.

These are the ones who have been summoned.

Five agree, one refuses. He doesn't want to lose any overtime. So there's a gap.

Can I go as the sixth?

The director shakes his head: a reporter as a pallbearer? A hell of a mess.

*

This empty road, this wreck of a truck, this air without a wisp of breeze.

This coffin.

Zieja wipes his oily hands with a rag. 'So what next?' he asks. 'We were supposed to be there this evening.'

We are stretched out on the edge of a ditch, on grass coated with a patina of dust. Our backs ache, our legs hurt, our eyes sting. Sleep, uninvited, introduces itself: warm, companionable, ingratiating.

'We'll sleep, boys,' Wiśnia says weakly, and curls up into a ball.

'And so?' Zieja says, surprised. 'Are we just going to go to sleep? But what about that other one?'

He shouldn't have mentioned it. Embarrassed by the question, sleep becomes awkward, backs away. We lie there in the torment of our fatigue, and now we are also anxious and uncertain, staring dully into a sky where a silver school of stars is swimming. We have to make up our minds.

Woś says: 'Let's stay here till morning. In the morning one of us can go into town and borrow a tractor. There's no need to hurry. This isn't a bakery.'

Jacek says: 'We can't wait till morning. It would be better to get this over with quickly, as quickly as possible.'

Kotarski says: 'You know, what if we just picked him up and carried him? He was a little guy, and a good bit of him is still underneath that block of coal. It's not much of a load. The job will be done by noon.'

It's a crazy idea, but it's one everyone likes. Put your shoulder to the wheel. It's early evening, and there aren't more than fifteen kilometres to go. We'll make it for sure. Besides, there's something else. Crouching on the edge of the ditch, having overcome the first temptation of sleep, more and more we feel that with this coffin literally hanging above our heads we are keeping a vigil, here in the deep darkness, amid shadows and bushes and the silent, deaf horizon: the tension of waiting for the dawn would be unbearable. It would be better to go, better to lug him! Take some sort of action, move, talk, vanquish the silence emanating from the black box, prove to the world and ourselves, and above all to ourselves, that we belong to the realm of the living – in which he, nailed in, the stiff, is an intruder, an alien, a creature resembling nothing at all.

At the same time we find ourselves looking upon the task ahead – this arduous carrying – as a sort of offering to be presented to the deceased, so that he will leave us in peace, freeing us of his insistent, cruel, and stubborn presence.

This march with the coffin on our backs has got off to a rough start. Seen from this viewpoint, the world has shrivelled to a small segment: the pendulum legs of the man ahead, a black slice of ground, the pendulum of your own legs. With his vision confined to this meagre prospect, a man instinctively summons imagination to his aid. Yes, the body may be bound, but the mind remains free.

'Anybody that came along now and ran into us would sure make tracks.'

'Know what? The moment he starts moving, we drop him and take off.'

'I just hope it doesn't rain. If he gets waterlogged, he'll be heavy.'

But there is no sign of rain. The evening is warm and the enormous, clear sky soars above an earth that is asleep now except for the sound of the crickets and the rhythmic tramping of our steps.

'Seventy-three, seventy-four, seventy-five' – Kotarski is counting. At 200 steps, we change. Three move to the left, three to the right. Then the other way around. The edge of the coffin, hard and sharp, digs into our shoulders. We turn off the paved road onto a forest track, taking a short cut that passes near the shore of the lake. After an hour we haven't done more than three kilometres.

'Why is it,' Wiśnia wonders, 'that someone dies and instead of being buried in the ground he hangs around and wears everybody else out? Not only that. They all wear themselves out just so that he can hang around. Why?'

'I read somewhere,' Jacek says, 'that in the war, when the snow melted on the Russian battlefields, the hands of the dead would start to show, sticking straight up. You'd be going along the road and all you'd see would be the snow and these hands. Can you imagine, nothing else? A man, when he's finished, doesn't want to drop out of sight. It's people who hide him from their sight. To be left in peace, they hide him. He won't go on his own.'

'Just like this one of ours,' says Woś. 'He'd follow us round the world. All we have to do is take him along. I think we could even get used to it.'

'Why not?' Gruber quips from the back of the coffin. 'Everyone's always bearing some burden. A career for one, rabbits for another, a wife for a third. So why shouldn't we have him?'

'Don't speak ill of him, or he'll kick you in the ear,' Woś warns.

'He's not dangerous,' Gruber says softly. 'He's behaved himself so far. He must have been OK.'

But in fact we don't know what he was like. None of us ever laid eyes on him. Stefan Kanik, eighteen, died in an accident. That's all. Now we can add that he weighed around sixty kilos. A young, slender boy. The rest is a mystery, a guess. And now this is the riddle that has taken on such an unseen and unknown shape, this alien, this stiff, ruling six living men, monopolizing their thoughts, wearing out their bodies, and, in cold, impenetrable silence, accepting their tribute of renunciation, submission, and voluntary consent to such an oddly formed destiny.

'If he was a good guy, then you don't mind lugging him,' says Woś, 'but if he was a son of a bitch, into the water with him.'

What was he like? Can you establish such facts? Yes, certainly! We've been lugging him for about five kilometres and we've poured out a barrel of sweat. Haven't we invested a great deal of labour, of nerves, of our own peace of mind, into this remnant? This effort, a part of ourselves, passes on to the stiff, raises his worth in our eyes, unites us with him, our brother across the barrier between life and death. The feeling of mutual strangeness dwindles. He has become ours. We won't plop him into the water. Sentenced to a burden we feel increasingly keenly, we will fulfil, to the very end, our mission.

The forest ends at the edge of the lake. There is a little clearing. Woś calls for a rest and starts to make a bonfire.

*

The flame shoots up immediately, impudent and playful. We settle down in a circle and pull off our shirts, now wet and sour-smelling. In the wavering, pulsating glow we can see each other's sweating faces, glistening torsos and red, swollen shoulders. The heat spreads from the bonfire in concentric waves. We have to back away. Now the coffin is closest to the fire.

'We'd better move that piece of furniture before it starts to roast and begins stinking,' Woś says.

We pull the coffin back, push it into the bushes, where Pluta breaks off some branches and covers it up.

We sit down around the fire. We are still breathing heavily, fighting sleep and a feeling of unease, baking ourselves in the warmth and revelling in light miraculously conjured from the darkness. We begin to fall into a state of inertia, abandonment, numbness. The night has imprisoned us in a cell shut off from the world, from other beings, from hope.

Just at that moment we hear Wiśnia's high, terrifying whisper: 'Quiet. Something's coming!'

A sudden, unbearable spasm of terror. Icy pins stab into our backs. Against our will, we glance towards the bushes, in the direction of the coffin. Jacek can't take it: he presses his head into the grass and, exhausted, sleep-starved, suddenly afraid, he begins to weep. This brings us all to our senses. Woś comes to himself first and falls upon Jacek, pulling at him and then pummelling him. He beats him fiercely, until the boy's weeping turns to groans, to a low, drawn-out sigh. Woś backs off at last, leans on a stump, and ties his shoe.

In the meantime the voices that Wiśnia detected become distinct and draw closer. We can hear snatches of melody, laughter, shouts. We listen attentively. Amid this dark wilderness our caravan has found traces of mankind. The voices are quite close now. Finally we pick out the silhouettes. Two, three, five.

They're girls. Six, seven.

Eight girls.

The girls – at first afraid, uncertain – end up staying. As the conversation gets off the ground, they start settling down around the fire next to us, so close that we could reach out and put our arms around them. It feels good. After everything we've been through, after a day of hard travelling, an exhausting march, the nerve-wracking tension, after all of this, or perhaps in spite of all this, it feels good.

'Are you coming back from a hike, too?' they ask.

'Yes,' Gruber says, lying. 'Beautiful evening, isn't it?'

'Beautiful. I'm just starting to appreciate it. Like everyone.'

'Not everyone,' Gruber says. 'There are some who don't appreciate anything. Now or ever. Never.'

We're all watching the girls closely. In colourful dresses, their shoulders bare and sun-bronzed – in the flickering light golden and brown by turns – their eyes seemingly indifferent but in fact provocative and vigilant at the same time, accessible and unreachable, they stare into the blazing fire and appear to be surrendering to the strange and somewhat pagan mood that a night-time forest bonfire evokes in people. Looking upon these unexpected visitors we feel that, despite the numbness, sleepiness and exhaustion, we are slowly being filled with an inner warmth – and, while wanting it, we sense the danger that comes with it. The edifice that holds in place the purpose and justification for making this extraordinary effort on behalf of a dead man is suddenly tottering. Why bother? Who needs it when an opportunity like this presents itself? Only negative feelings link us to the dead man: in our new mood we could break away from the stiff so completely that any further toil of carrying the coffin would strike us as downright idiocy. Why make fools of ourselves?

Woś, however, has remained gloomy after the incident with Jacek, and has not joined in the flirting. He draws me aside.

'There's going to be trouble,' he whispers. 'One or the other of them is sure to go off after a skirt. And if we're a man short, we won't be able to carry the coffin. This could turn into a stupid hassle.'

From this remove, our calves almost touching the sides of the coffin, we watch the scene in the clearing. Gruber will go for sure. Kotarski, Pluta – no. And Jacek? He's a question mark. He is, at heart, a shy boy, and wouldn't initiate a thing unless the girl made the first move: he'd turn tail at her first 'No.' Yet because his character affords him few chances, he would grab avidly if one presented itself.

'It's a dead cert Jacek goes,' Woś says.

'Let's get back to the fire,' I tell him. 'We're not going to solve anything here.'

We return. Pluta has thrown on some more wood. 'Remember, it was autumn,' the girls are singing. We feel good, and we feel uneasy. No one has breathed a word about the coffin, but the coffin is still there. Our awareness of its existence, of its paralysing participation, makes us different from the girls.

Stefan Kanik, eighteen. Someone who is missing and at the same time is the most present. Reach out and you can put your arm around a girl; take a few steps and you can lean over the coffin – we are standing between life at its most beautiful and death at its most cruel.

The stiff came to us unknown, and for that reason we

can easily identify him with every boy in the world we have ever happened to meet. Yes, that was the one, that one for sure. He was standing in the window in an unbuttoned checked shirt, watching the cars drive past, listening to the babble of conversations, looking at the passing girls – the wind blowing out their full skirts, uncovering the whiteness of their starched slips, so stiff that you could stand them up on the floor like haystacks. And then he went out into the street and met his own girl and walked with her, buying her sweets and the most expensive lemon soda – Moorish Delight – and then she bought him strawberries and they went to the movie *Holiday With Monica*, in which an actress with a difficult name undresses in front of an actor with a difficult name, which his girl has never done in front of him, not even once. And afterwards he kissed her in the park, watching from out of the corner of his eye from behind her head, through her careless loose hair, to make sure that a policeman wasn't coming who would take down his name and send him to school, or would want twenty zloty when they didn't have more than five between them. And afterwards the girl would say: 'We have to go now', but she wouldn't get up from the park bench; she would say: 'Come on, it's late', and she would cuddle against him more tightly, and he would ask: 'Do you know how butterflies kiss?' and move his eyelids close to her cheek and flutter them, which must have tickled her, because she would laugh.

Perhaps he would meet her many more times, but in our minds that naive and banal image was the only and the final one, and afterwards we saw only what we had never wanted to see, ever, until the last day of our lives.

And when we pushed away that other, bad vision, we felt good again and everything was a joy to us: the fire, the smell of trampled grass, that our shirts had dried, the sleep of the earth, the taste of cigarettes, the forest, our rested legs, the stardust, life – life most of all.

In the end, we went on. The dawn met us. The sun warmed us. We kept walking. Our legs buckled, our shoulders went numb, our hands swelled, but we managed to carry it to the cemetery – to the grave – our last harbour on earth, at which we put in only once, never again to sail forth – this Stefan Kanik, eighteen, killed in a tragic accident, during blasting, by a block of coal.